# THE MIME SPEAKS

## NATE THE MIME

Blue Heron Book Works, LLC

Allentown, Pennsylvania

ISBN: ISBN: 978-1-7354019-1-1
https://www.natethemime.com/
Cover design by Angie Zambrano
Cover photo by Paul Heller
Blue Heron Book Works, LLC
Allentown, Pennsylvania 18104
www.blueheronbookworks.com

*I dedicate this book to my sister, Nita Moran, for always being there for me. Not only is she my sister, she's my best friend. Love you with all my heart, your big, little brother.*

# TABLE OF CONTENTS

# ACKNOWLEDGMENTS

I thank everyone for all the love and support you give me. Much love and respect. Never give up, and always bring a smile.

# CHAPTER 1
The Proclamation

*"We recognize an outstanding individual, one worthy of the esteem of both the Village of Harlem and the great State of New York."*

Let me tell you a story. It was a beautiful summer day in July 2019. I was in Harlem doing a community event for Silent Cry Non-Profit, which is a positive force in the community. They're against gun violence. they advocate for bringing the older and younger generations together as well as providing outlets outside of school to develop children's minds and helping them imagine a life beyond their neighborhood. It was a block party with food and vendors, and one that I had performed at several times before. When I believe in something I don't mind working for free. And Silent Cry Non-Profit is something I believe in. Kids were running around having fun. The neighborhood church allowed people to use their bathroom. The whole block was involved. It was like an ordinary gig, except that day I was lucky enough to get a parking spot right in the block. I changed my clothes in the car, as usual. I'm kind of like Superman like that. I go in Nate Moran and come out Nate the Mime, ready to dance and make you smile. The party was just getting started when I got out of the car. You could smell the great food. Vendors were passing out giveaways to the kids, backpacks. Other vendors and organizations had stuff for the community. I danced a piece called "Khalid: Talk" then I moved through the crowd and interacted with the people, making them smile. After all the performers did their thing, the emcee started calling people to the dais to get awards and proclamations for the good things they did for the community. I think I was eating a slice of pizza when Silent Cry called me up to the podium. "Nate the Mime! Come up here." I was frozen in place because I certainly didn't expect to be getting anything. And I certainly wasn't prepared for what the presenter said. "You deserve much more. We appreciate all that you do for us in the community." She read the proclamation aloud for all the people and I was stunned.

**"Significant contributions to the community embody the character that inspires us all and is truly the lifeblood of the community."**

I was speechless. And yes, tears formed in my eyes. It was a proclamation from the state of New York signed by State Senator Brian Benjamin.

**"Nate has been a dancer all his life, performing all around the world."**

I was overwhelmed. They took pictures of us together, so I know it happened! I also have the official Proclamation which I'm showing you here. I couldn't believe it. The presenter read on:

*"He is also a former homeless veteran. Eleven years ago, he was homeless for two years on the streets of New York. Now he pushes the message to Never Give Up!"*

That last part is what made it unbelievable. Eleven years ago, I had been homeless for two years on the streets of New York. I don't know how many people who were there that day listening to my Proclamation knew what it meant to live on the streets, to get up every day between two other homeless guys in a row of homeless guys sleeping on the sidewalk, waiting for each other to get up and get that first fifth of whiskey before being chased by the police. I don't know how many people who were there that day understood how high a climb it is from the bottom to the first step out. Yeah, it feels good when you finally reach a small goal on your way to the big prize, but there are lots of steps to the top and they are all hard and each one is an excuse to go back to square one. I know. I've been there and I understand all too well the phrase "one step forward, two steps back," but I have managed to balance on a top step for eleven years. My instinct is to keep looking forward. I never look back to the bottom. Cause I still have lots to do. My dream is to buy a big warehouse and fix it up so artists who don't have a place to do their art have a place to go. If they can give me $5 that's cool. Money doesn't mean anything to me except as a means to an end. I want to leave a legacy. I always say in my acts, "Never Give Up!" I think that mantra is what kept me going forward. It certainly wasn't Atta boys or someone giving me a prize if I didn't mess up. You got to find a way to reward yourself for not messing up, for staying on track. A reward that doesn't involve the stuff that got you to the bottom in the first place.

Shawanna Erena Vaughn, from *Silent Cry,* a non-profit organization, facilitated me being awarded the proclamation. Here we are at the Apollo theater in NYC.

But sometimes, it's encouraging when someone notices that you aren't giving up and you're trying to make a difference in other people's lives. And that's why it moved me to receive that Proclamation. So I can tell you, when the going gets tough, you have to find that thing you love to do, that thing that defines you—whether it's music or art or taking care of animals—and that is the thing that will sustain you, that will get you through. I remember the warm applause of the people in the audience that day. I remember thinking that the applause was nice, but it's what you think of yourself that really matters.

I had a job for a while taking care of the county cemetery when I was in the VA. When I got back to the VA at night, I would bench press. Keep in shape. Do push-ups while looking at a sign that said, "this too shall pass." I just kept looking at that sign. Increasing reps. Increasing weight. And I never gave up.

I framed the Proclamation and it's in my office at home. Of course, it is!

# CHAPTER 2

Never Give Up

Like most people, I would like to say that my life had been perfect. That I had been perfect. That I always made good choices.

But I didn't, and I'm not.

But remember, my motto is "Never Give Up!" So, I'm still here and able to tell my story. I'm not real proud of some parts of my life, but I want you know that no matter what obstacles you face it's possible to overcome them. It's still possible to become who you want to be. What's the secret? That's right: Never Give Up!

When I first moved to New York, I was hanging with people in the streets and partying. I was basically living with my uncle. Then one day I was at a relative's house over the holidays and they said, "Oh, you got to try this eggnog" and I said no man, I can't do that. But they pushed me, and I did. And then I was back on beer and smoking weed. I was still functioning. But then, I started buying more smiles, paying fewer bills. My uncle put me out, and I was out on the street.

I admitted myself to Kings County Hospital to clean up my act. Get sober. It was a program in the Bowery in Manhattan. You get your own place. When I finished that program, I got my own room in East New York and got back on my feet. Seven years I was on my own. I was selling photo packages with a national photography company and training others to be salespeople. Then me and the boss locked horns, and I got a job through a temp company working for Ernst and Young, which I liked. But then the boss came back to me and offered me a management position in the company. I'm a very good salesman. That's how I met my wife. I was selling pictures. This woman comes in and I'm thinking—and saying, too!—This is the most beautiful woman I have ever seen! I give her my number and say, "give me a call. Can I walk you to the train station?" I did. I walked her to the train station under an umbrella. I called her every day. We had our first dinner in an Indian restaurant in the village. Pretty soon, we got to the point where she was making dinner for me every night.

Then I moved in. Our lives got comfortable and we had a beautiful daughter. But things fell apart.

The first time I landed, when I was in Kings County Hospital, I was the same old Nate, carrying the same old me around. Looking for money to "buy me a smile." That's right, a drink. I'd buy a smile before I paid my bills. I was seven years clean. I had my own apartment, my own car. But that couldn't compete with a drink.

So, I landed back in the streets again. There were some moments that weren't all bad, though. Once, some guy, I never saw him before or since, looked at my shoes, which were pretty awful, and he said, we got to get you out of those. What size shoe do you wear? I told him and he came back a little later with a brand-new pair of British shoes. He said, put em on! I threw the old ones away and put on the new ones. It made me feel different. I never saw that guy again. But I never forgot how he made me feel, when he bought me these beautiful shoes and it changed how I saw myself. I still have those shoes. You always have to surround yourself with people who believe you're awesome. This is what I'm talking about.

My daughter, Natalie, was living on Long Island and it was her birthday. I wanted to see her, so I called her, and she agreed to see me.

I went to the Salvation Army and got a coat, it was a girl's coat, but it kept me warm. I went to the barber school for a haircut.

Then I saw my daughter. We were glad to see each other, we hugged, then she had to go. It made me feel sad at how my life was going. So, of course, I went to the liquor store and got a pint. When I was going into the E street station, a lady with a baby carriage asked me to open the gate for her and when she went in, I said, well, the door's open I might as well go in after her, save some change, and that's when the cops caught me. They ran a check on me and found out I had outstanding warrants for DUI, so they took me in. That was in Nassau County.

I had a lot of warrants out for DUI. So, when I got picked up, they found all my old warrants. I tried to charm the female police—I got a thing for women in uniforms—but they found my warrants and I landed in Carmen Avenue, the county jail for Nassau County.

They locked me up because I had so many outstanding warrants. At first, they wanted to give me 12 months, then the judge reduced it to 10 months and then finally to 6 months.

In jail, I couldn't sleep. They started watching me and giving me pills to sleep. I told them I didn't want to get into the pill thing because I was already an alcoholic. I told them: I know you have a program for alcoholics, and I want to join that. I wanted to get rid of that taste, you see. So, they let me into the program. I was put into a wing for addicts and alcoholics, we had prayer sessions, meetings. I started helping them serve food as a job, which was a step up. And there was a gym and I would do my exercises in front of the mirror with a sign that says, "This too shall pass."

I got moved into the kitchen where I served food and I prayed with these guys. And our prayers went something like this:

"Lord, help me with this situation that I'm in, because I know you'll never leave me or forsake me."

And always, I thought, "This too shall pass."

I still have that over the mirror in my office. This too shall pass. No matter how bad things are, they will get better.

Ultimately, I was in for four months. But it killed two birds with one stone: it cleared my warrants and it got me sober.

When I got out, I heard the Salvation Army on Long Island, Northport had a program for Veterans. They told me they had places in Manhattan, but I didn't want to be in Manhattan, you know? I didn't want to be around the people and places that triggered me to want to drink. When I got out, they wanted to put me in the city, New York, but I said, I wanted to go to Northport, Long Island. I wanted to go to the Veterans Administration. I didn't even have any clothes.

I could tell you lots of stories of what it's like on the street, but I'll just tell you a few. I would like to think the stories would be so scary, it would help you make better choices, but I know better. Especially if you're trapped by drugs or alcohol, then those things make the choices for you.

But here's the thing: I want to inspire you! And sometimes, the way to inspire people is to show what you went through, so they're inspired to do better!

I WANT TO INSPIRE PEOPLE.

I want to let people know that whatever you go through, no matter what happens, you can get through it. Because I've been through some stuff! You wouldn't believe some of the stuff that's happened to me. A lot of it happened to me when I was homeless, because when you're homeless you're out there, 24/7.

Once, when I was sleeping on the street on a park bench, I woke up to kids throwing 40s (beer bottles) at me.

Another time, I was at Windgate Park, I woke up with a guy with dreadlocks hitting me in the face. I came out swinging. But I got beat pretty badly. I ran to a gas station where they knew me, and they gave me peroxide and band aids.

Once, I was at Ebbetts Field Projects on the 26th floor, trying to sleep on top of the roof. Guys with baseball bats drove me off. You don't know how fast you can run until you have to run down 26 flights of steps with guys chasing you with baseball bats!

I can't blame anyone for the stuff that happened to me, I was mostly hanging with the wrong people.

For instance, in New York, I was drinking wine and smoking weed with this woman and she said, let's go to my friend's house. He's Jamaican. So, we went to his house, in the basement, and she said she had to go to the bathroom or something. Anyway, she didn't come back. The Jamaican guy came downstairs and he said, what's going on? I said I was waiting for his friend, and the Jamaican guy said, she left. So, I said, well, I'd better leave too. And the Jamaican guy said, you owe me money for using my basement and I said, I don't got any money. He said, "what about that watch?" and he took my watch and said, "what else you got?" He let me call a friend, but the friend said, "I don't have any money," so the Jamaican guy told his friends, "tie him up" and they tied me up with some electrical wire. And he got a machete and he started paddling me with it, and said, "I'm going to cut you in half and leave your body out back and no one's going to find it until you start to smell." And then he let me call another friend who wired some money to this guy via Western Union and he let me go. Then when I was walking away, the guy said, "hey, where you going? Why don't you come back and hang with us?"

Come back and hang with us?

You can see how crazy life on the streets is. That's why I don't recommend it! You can't be a positive influence if you are worried about some madman threatening to cut you in half with a machete, or guys pelting you awake with beer bottles.

Are you inspired yet? Because you know, I've slept in every kind of place. I've slept in houses where babies had the same diaper on for days. I've slept in places where the only food in the house was one green hotdog in the refrigerator. You don't even *know*. I've slept in places where every other word is a curse word.

I know that some of you did, too. Right? And some of us get up, and some of us stay down. What makes a person get up? Because people ask me that all the time, they say, "Nate, why did you keep getting up, after you've been knocked down so many times?"

This is my answer: "Cause I know it wasn't me on the floor. I wasn't raised to be in that situation." No matter how poor you were raised, if there was a strong adult in your life, your mama, your grandma, your grandpa, you KNOW that you don't belong on the floor."

But here's a secret: even if you didn't have that kind of support when you were young, it's never too late to get it. What do I say? Never give up! Never give up looking for people to get in your life who see you as the awesome human being you are. When you surround yourself with those people, people who believe in you, you can start to believe that you can always pick yourself up off the floor as well.

And sometimes, you know, it can get so bad that it can only go one way and that way is up! The next day had to be a better day. If it's getting bad, sometimes the old lightbulb comes on and you realize, "this isn't where I'm supposed to be! I'm supposed to be somewhere better." And that's when the miracles start. When the doors start to open.

Once, I was panhandling in front of a liquor store in Freeport, Long Island. I wanted some liquor bad and this man coming into the store said, "I know what you want the money for. But, you have to do something for me first. I want you to say this prayer, 'Lord, Take this taste from my mouth'."

So, I said it, cause we're talking about a bottle. And he says, say it slower. And I did. It didn't mean anything to me at the time, I just wanted the liquor, but I started saying the prayer all the time. I could be putting liquor in my mouth while peeling off my socks, and all I had left was this prayer. And I said it, and I said it.

Now, some people talk about affirmations and such. And I know this: you are what you say you are. You get what you ask for. Whatever comes out of your mouth goes out into the universe, it goes to God, and it comes back to you in the form of blessings and love.

And so, when I said this little prayer, "Lord, take this taste from my mouth," over and over, soon I started to mean it. I wanted the taste of liquor gone from my life and then, not right away maybe, but soon, it was gone.

I want to inspire people because I don't want anyone to feel the pain I did.

Somebody asked me once, how can you be so happy? They knew that I cleaned up at the Sands Casino. They said, you got to pick up all the dirt and believe me, I did. I even once saw a lady poop in the corner, and I had to clean that up. But they don't know what I had seen and done before. I mean, I had a guy standing over with me a knife who wanted to cut my eye out! Yeah, I will clean up the dirt at the Sands any day. I'm happy to do it.

The second time was harder. Different crowd, different energy. I surrendered myself to the streets.

Till I got tired of seeing myself in the streets.

One basic thing and you're out. You got to be ready.

I want to inspire people.

My big dream is to buy a big building where artists can come and

 do their art. I don't care if they give me 5, 10 bucks or whatever. Come in and do your thing. I don't think people shouldn't be doing their thing because they don't have a place to do it. That's crazy, right? I want to have enough money to make a difference in peoples' lives. A big building where artists could come and do their thing is one thing I would do with a lot of money. The other thing is, I would love to give big tips to waitresses and waiters. Not 20%, but a tip that was big enough so they could go home after their shift and say to their family, "You wouldn't believe what happened to me today! This guy gave me this money and now we can_____" You fill in the blanks. Wouldn't that be the best feeling in the world to be able to make that kind of a difference in someone's life?

It's okay to inspire people that I know, people that I come in contact with. Another dream I have is I want to be on television to inspire more people in the world. So, more people can hear what I'm saying.

Television is the way to reach a LOT of people at once. I want to inspire you. But that doesn't mean I'm better than you. Not at all. I'm the guy who used to buy shoes at Payless and wore them until they got holes in the soles. Which means that I was walking on newspapers a lot to cover up the holes in the soles. I've been there. However down you've been, me too! And I picked myself up. And I  want to inspire you to do the same.

Who inspires me? All the greats. Tyler Perry, I want to sit down and have a cup of coffee with him. Oprah, Steve Harvey, Obama, and anyone who's doing great things for the world.

# CHAPTER 3

Your Juice!

I always liked to dance. It's in my bones, in my blood. It is my blood, it's my juice! Ya'll got your own juice. It could be dancing, but it could be singing, or writing or painting. Or even listening to music. Or working on your car. But it's your juice. It's the thing you do when you're sad. The thing you do when you hit the wall. Your passion! What your heart desires. Your juice will carry you through any storm. I was born in 1961 and raised in Virginia in the country by my grandmother who raised 13 grandchildren. I was the youngest of all the grandchildren. We were very poor, my grandmother did everything herself, but as I said earlier, when you're a child, if you have an adult in your life who thinks you're awesome, you have a good shot at life.

I was on the JROTC drill team at JFK High School. It was my first experience with dance, with movement. We were given poles at first to twirl, then M-1s and finally M-14s. We practiced 2 hours a day. And then I walked home. The weather was either too hot or too cold for twirling. Your hands were either too cold or burning up. We did the death line. You swung your pole and the person next to you ducked. And so on down the line.

We were so good we went to the nationals in Washington, D.C. Every year I went. Other times we traveled to Texas to compete. San Antonio. Most of the kids were Spanish. Boy were they good. One kid, Pierre, always won the Individual Fancy Drill. They told me I was to compete against him. He was sharp. Everything was tick, tick, tick. Very precise. I love precision. That's why I love Eminem. He's precise. I like to give it justice when I drop it.

Anyway, I did compete against Pierre, and I took 3$^{rd}$ place. I did my robot moves. I remember I threw the pole in the air, and it took so long to come down, I had time to talk to myself.

Colonel Chapman was our officer in JROTC. Despite the fact that my father wasn't in the military, I had some uncles who were and, because of my experience on the JROTC drill team, I guess I always figured I would join the military, which I did when I was 18.

I didn't like school. In fact, I didn't graduate. My last year of school, my first class in the morning was supposed to be government, but I went to a girlfriend's house. "Girlfriend class" if you know what I mean. She gave me a bag of weed, and we hung out when everyone else was learning about government.

I say it like it's funny, but I have to say that not graduating high school was always a big thing in my life. Whenever you fill out an application for a job or a mortgage, that box that says "high school graduate" gets bigger and bigger because you can't put a check mark there. It becomes larger than life. And, I must admit, more than once I was tempted to lie, to check that box. But I couldn't. My advice here is, if you don't want that unchecked box to take over your life, stay in school and graduate.

But, at the time, I didn't care that I didn't graduate, because I knew I was going straight to the army. I was delayed entry. My MOS (Military Occupational Specialty) was 05C Communications, teletype operator. I was a PFC. They molded us.

I was eventually stationed in Europe. My future dance partner and I flew in from Jersey together, although we didn't know at the time that either of us danced. We were stationed together in Heidelberg (and later Mannheim), and one night after we had a couple in the Enlisted Men's Club (EMC), we had on some music and he started dancing. Then I started dancing. And we looked at each other and said, "whoooo!"

"I didn't know you could do that," he said.

"I didn't know you could do that," I answered.

We were all ticks and pops. He was Pee Wee. We started doing routines together as the Poppeters. At wine fests and beer fests. We were a big hit. Crowd roaring approval. They did articles on us in the papers.

When I was in Basic Training, my drill sergeant would take me to the EM Club and put money on me, saying I could out-dance anyone in the club, but I didn't think it would go over well if our chain-of-command in Germany knew about our dancing and we tried to keep it secret, but it was hard when we were in the newspaper. And sure enough, finally, our captain heard about what was happening and called us in. We thought, "this is it," he was going to ask us to quit, but he said we could keep doing it as long as we said we represented the 97th

Signal Corp. It was good. I was using my juice again, you know what I mean? Can't slow me down.

My ex-wife and I lived off post in Hemsbach, about 30 minutes from Mannheim. We had a passionate relationship. She would come to the shows where PeeWee and me were dancing, but she would get jealous. Not that I was doing anything wrong. Cause I wasn't. But some women, when they saw me on stage, would say to her, "Wow, sister, does he move like that in bed?" and sometimes they would give me their phone numbers that I would just put in my pocket. I never called any of them. But she would find the phone numbers later and get mad. I don't blame her, but it didn't make for a peaceful existence. And I didn't quit dancing because, it's my juice, right?

We managed to stay together until we transferred to Colorado.

I moved out. That's when I started drinking heavy. I stopped dancing. It was the worst thing I could do. Remember what I said? When you hit the wall, you got to use your juice. Well, I didn't use my juice. I started drinking really heavily instead.

Before we got divorced, I said, let me get out of the Army, you stay in. She had more time in service and more time in grade, so it made sense for her to stay. After we got divorced, I lost contact with my older daughter for a long time, although with God's grace it seems to be improving.

I already told you how I hit bottom with drinking, homelessness. When I got sober, I promised myself that I would never stop dancing again. The only thing that'll stop is me being in that box.

# CHAPTER 4
Put Your Best Foot forward

I'm a salesman, I sold everything. I'm a *good* salesman. I *kicked* it!

I think it's because I love working with people.

I sold photo packages for A&S department store, which later became Macy's, in New York.

I sold advertising for a radio station. I'm driving in my car in California and I hear an ad: they need salesmen to sell airtime. So, I got dressed up and went to apply for the job, and they gave me the territory from Monterey to Carmel. The station was KIDD/KWEST 630 AM radio station in Montery. It's not easy to sell radio advertising because you can't guarantee a return, in fact, as a salesman, I could only guarantee when their ad would play. So, it's a tough sell.

One of my clients was the Mercedes Benz dealership. I went in and there was no wall or door on the manager's office, his desk was kind of out in the open, and when I spoke to him, he said, "don't you knock? Get out of here!"

So, I went back to my supervisor and told him what happened, and he said, "Go back!" so, I did. This time I knocked on the wall, and the manager said, "You again! I thought I told you to get out of here."

So, I told my supervisor again what happened, and he said, "Go back!" and I said, "Whaaaa?" But I did. The manager this time said, "You AGAIN! All right, tell me what you want." And now, I'm thinking, this guy put me through so much, I'm going to sell him the DELUX package. And I did.

I made a lot of money on that job. I made a thousand a month plus 20% commission. That was way back then. One of the big things that selling taught me was persistence and always showing up for the gig. A friend of mine who sells real estate told me: it takes twenty-five "no's" to get to a "yes." So, I always look at a no as just a step on my way to yes.

But I think the most important thing is, no matter how humble the job, I always tried to put my best foot forward. I always tried to do the best I could. You never know when someone's watching to see what you can do, and besides, every job you have has a contract. You will do this job which entails this and this, and they will pay you. It's a deal. And it's your *word*.

When I was out in the street, I kept hearing "you're a bum" and "get a job" and it didn't sit right with me. And even then I was always looking for ways to get out there.

If you know Brooklyn, let me tell you the location so you can get the visual of exactly where I was at. On Nostrand Avenue and Sterling Street, there's a Johnny pump there on the corner, and across the street was Mama's Chicken. Sitting around and drinking beer with fellas on the corner, we were hitting ideas around on how to make money. Finally, we decided that if we open this Johnny pump, get some buckets, get some old rags, some Ivory soap, put a sign up "Five Dollars a Car Hand Wash" and well, let's see what happens. I had someone with me. What happened, the guy across the street at Mama's Chicken, he was a good sort, he didn't talk to me like a homeless guy, he just talked to me like another regular guy in the street. He took a liking to me. I told him my idea, and he said, "I have some buckets in the basement, you can get those, and I have some rags you can use."

So, he gave me the bucket, he gave me some old rags. I went to the 99cent store and got some Ivory soap, a toothbrush, and a little scrub pad. And he had a tool that he used to open the Johnny pump for the kids to play in the water when it got hot, and we turned it into a car wash. I put the sign up. The guy with me worked for one day, made some money and that was it. Back to the streets. But I looked at it as an opportunity for money, so I put the sign up, "Five Dollars a Car" and opened up the pump and stood there and before you know it, cars are coming up. It was hot, washing those cars, detailing and washing the insides, it started getting really busy and the neighbors were noticing, calling me "Car Wash," "Yo, what's up Car Wash?" I treated it like a job. I get up in the morning, early bird gets the worm they say, and I'm already out in the street. You can sleep right on the corner and come right back and be on time.

I would go to the Johnny pump and open up at 6 in the morning, 7 days a week, and shut down sometime at 5 or 6 then I would go somewhere else and drink, even though my friends would come. It turned into a hang out spot sometimes, too. Those guys would sit there drinking and watch me wash cars. Sometimes, I would be washing three cars at a time. I would have one car around the corner, soap it up, run back, soap another one, soap another one, running back and forth to the point where people could see how hard I was working. I turned so black being out in the sun, you know they say, "so black you blue," that was me. That corner got so busy that a limousine company gave me a contract, set me up for every Saturday to wash their limousines. They would pull up one at a time, and I guarantee they would give me 20, 30 dollars a car even though I still had the $5 sign up. This went on and on. It was a good deal, I'm telling you, man. I would leave, go party or whatever, away from that area. Friends were sitting on crates and stuff, and sometimes I had to tell them calm down, 'cause they would get loud and when the alcohol hit it would get louder. So I'd tell them, man, you'd better go around the corner with that, this is where I make my money, so you get too loud, the neighbors ain't going to like that, mess my business up.

It went on for a while. Then one day, a cop pulled up and he said, "Are you paying taxes for this water?" and I said, "Excuse me? I'm homeless, man, I'm just trying to survive, brother. I'm not out here hurting anybody. I'm just out here washing cars. Making a living for myself while I'm out here." People were leaning out the windows. Anyone who knows Brooklyn, knows people lean out the windows. They were hollering, "Leave Car Wash alone! He ain't bothering nobody. Let him get his money, he ain't bothering nobody." The police didn't hear none of that. He snatched my sign down, kicked my bucket over, and turned the water hose off and he pulled off. As soon as he pulled off, I put my sign back up. What's he going to do? Give me three hots and a cot? I put my sign back up, turned the water hose back on, filled my bucket back up, suds it up, get ready for the next car that's coming. And it went on for a while. Until I got tired. Remember, I told you I was homeless twice. And I did that until I went to Kings County to detox out. So I stayed there, washed cars, partied, and came back. It was like a cycle. Like a seven day cycle. I made money. But I didn't hear anybody say, "Get a job, bum" "Get out of my face, why you got no money? Look at you, you stinking!" No one knew I was homeless in the neighborhood, they considered me "Car Wash."

It's crazy. I went over to my old neighborhood yesterday and I drove through there to look at the Johnny pump, to remember where I came from, and I wondered if Maxine, my friend, still lived around here. And outdoors she came. I said, "Woooowwww, Sis. It's crazy. I wondered if you were still living here. You remember me?" She said, "I know you, Nate. I blocked those spaces many times so you could wash cars there. I remember you."

I told her what I was doing, working on a book and changing my life, moved out of New York. She said, "I'm proud of you. There was something about you."

We took a picture together with the masks on. I was so excited I put my mask on upside down.

You know what's crazy? When I wash my car now, it's like, "Man, I'm washing *my* car!" When I used to wash the cars, I didn't like to look in the mirror because I didn't like what I saw. I didn't like who I was. I cleaned them, but I turned my head away. Now when I wash my car, I look in that mirror. I can look in any mirror. I say thank you. I take pride in myself. Sometimes, when I was homeless, I would go to the gas station and pump gas to try to make money. "Excuse me, Miss, can I pump your gas?" The second time I was homeless, I would go to the gas station, and try to pump gas for people. When it got good, I kept on going. Might leave, but I didn't want to leave for a minute because I might miss something. It's like in sales, you can either have a slow morning and a fast afternoon, or a fast morning and a slow afternoon. So, once I got rolling, and people were giving me money to pump their gas, I didn't want to leave, because I didn't want to miss anything. So, when it died down, I faded off. Or until the attendant said, "You got to leave buddy, because someone complained." So, then I go to another gas station and do that same thing. Just like, you know the Spanish guys, they go to Home Depot and line up for jobs? Well, I used to go to Home Depot in Freeport, Long Island and I would go and stand with the Spanish guys, but I would help people load their cars up. Putting my best foot forward. "Excuse me, can I help you load your car up? Put the wood on?"

They had people with aprons working inside, but I was outside hustling. Trying to get to a yes. Eventually, someone would say, "Come on, brother, I see you're trying to make some money. Load up my car for me." And that's what I would do. Load up their cars with wood, bricks, cement. Sometimes they even took me on a job, because I speak English. They would take me on a job, a couple hundred dollars a day, because I spoke English.

And then there was Christmas. Oh my God. Christmas! Christmas trees! Everybody buys Christmas trees. So, what I would do, I would wait, get my string together, just like I worked there. "Excuse me, ma'm, tie your tree up?" I was on it. I was so used to working growing up, chopping wood, doing chores, work was no problem for me. Out there, you got to figure out how you're going to pay for things. But I wasn't focused. I didn't sit back and say, "This is my way out." I just looked at it like, "I'm hustling." So, I kept on, tying trees down. Even though I didn't have a plan, I always tried to do my best. I think it was practice for doing what I really wanted to do.

The thing I was slowly learning, though, is you have to have a plan. Otherwise, you're at the mercy of everything. I met a guy today. Dude is sleeping in his car. Dude has plans. He has a great thing to go for. He said, Hey man, I'm glad I met you. You give me hope. He said, give me a hug. Even with this pandemic going on, I gave him a hug. I see him making it, because he has a plan. I see him making something miraculous because he has a plan. That was what I was about to learn.

This is the story of me, not having a plan. Of running and running on the treadmill until I was pushed off. You know, sometimes you're putting your best foot forward, doing the best you can, giving 110% and it still doesn't work out the way you plan? But then, it works out for the better. Let me tell you how it happened.

I had moved from New York to Pennsylvania, and I was working Target from four in the morning till about eight. I didn't have a car. Because being from New York, you don't need a car! Pennsylvania forced me to get a car because I was taking a taxi to work every morning and for four hours, I was hustling just to get the money to get to work!

So, I applied to Sands Casino and I was very grateful to get the job. I was cleaning. Cigarette butts, saliva. Even poop. One guy says to me, "Oh, man, you got the worst job! Why are you always smiling and happy, man?" And I say, "I'm thankful to have a job." A lot of managers, supervisors, gave me compliments on how hard I worked, because I gave 110%. Because when I walked through those doors, I was Sands Casino. They asked me to do a job, I said, "Let's go!" Because, if you're signing that check, I work for you. And I signed a contract saying what I would do. It's like a gig. I sign a contract saying I'll do this song and that song. You sign that paper, that's your obligation. It's not your obligation to go in a corner and hide!

I put that kind of work in for the Sands. I had people say, "Slow down, man. You're making me look bad!

Anybody that knew me from Sands, knows I'm telling the truth. I was good at customer service. I'm not bragging. I'm just telling you that's what I was doing. I had the night shift, 11 to 7. Mondays and Tuesdays off. I was still able to slide some gigs in because I was working with someone. We could switch days off. It worked like that for a while. It got to the point that *Amsterdam Magazine* did an article on me, going from being homeless to performing.

Sands Casino got wind of it because one of my co-workers said I should put it on the personnel board. I said, no, I don't want people to know I was homeless, but they said, no, it shows character.

After Sands saw the article, *they* did an article on me, "We got a star among us." So now, everybody in Sands knew I was a performer. I still did work. I didn't use that to get over.

Even the high jack. Some people were scared of heights, but I wasn't. I was using the high jack to clean vents in the ceiling all the way to the top. I worked extra hard. I even worked 2 in the morning to 10 in the morning. I cleaned toilets, I stripped floors, I shampooed carpets. I hauled trash. There was so much trash, you couldn't even see me between the two hand trucks. I gave them everything that I had.

Once I did get home, I was finished. But then I got up the next day and did it again. It is what it is. That's the way I am. I can't feel right, knowing I signed a contract to do this and that and then I shammed. I gave a 110%. I go back to the Casino and people say, "We miss you!" head managers, people like that.

This is what happened with them.

Everyone in the Casino knew I was a performer. But they also knew I was a hard worker. So, the time comes I want to do the show with the National Veterans Creative Arts Festival. They send tickets for your flight and pay for your hotels. I already told you this. And I was invited to go.

So, this event comes up. I go to my supervisors and tell them I got to be in Buffalo for the whole week, everything's already paid for. I told them *way* in advance. I have 4 days, I need 3 more days. They said, go ahead. We'll take care of it.

So, I follow my dreams and go to Buffalo.

But when I came back, I felt something. You know I heard a voice. Something didn't feel right. That Friday, I got called into the Human Resource office. I was let go. I had put my best foot forward, I had given 110% and still, I was let go.

But it was time to go for my dreams. Sometimes, you need a push. By them releasing me and letting me go, it was the push I needed to go for my dreams. I said, 'You know what? I don't want to work for anyone, I want to be independent. And so far, the Lord is blessing me. All my bills are paid. I don't have a lot of money like some people, but my bills are paid, I'm still eating, I still have clothes on my back. At least I'm following my dream.

It was like you're hanging on to your mama's aprons, you got to let go. When I went into the army my Grandma said, "I hate to see you go, but I'm glad you're leaving."

Now, so many doors have opened. When it's time to go for your dream, go for it. Sometimes, some doors close so others can open. Even now when I go back to the Casino, and it's been three and a half years, they ask me when I'm coming back. That's because I gave my all. Now I'm giving my all to my dream.

Performing for Mardi Gras Chamber of Commerce at the Sands Event Center

# CHAPTER 5

## Finding My Footing

Michael Peterson and Jill Peterson, Country Western Singer, Jill is an ex-Lt. Col. In the Army. He hosts the National Veteran Creative Arts festival every year.

This is how I got to the Salvation Army to get my life together. It was the biggest, most powerful move of my life. They sent a van to Comet Avenue, Nassau County Jail, the day I walked out of that jail. I had cleared all my DUIs that I owed in NY. I didn't have the money, so I did the time for all the fines I had to pay. They gave me a shiny bullet though. But, when I walked through that door, I was cleared. Everything was done. All my debts were cleared, and I didn't have to go back to court.

They sent a van to pick me up at the County Jail to take me to Comet Avenue. When I got in that van, I knew there was something about it. Straight to Northport, LI, the Salvation Army. All I had was the clothes on my back, the little piece of property they give you when you leave. It was all I had to my name. I walked in the door, they greeted me with a smile and hugs, sent me to in-processing at the Veteran's Administration to get my ID. One thing about veterans, no matter how high or low you are, we are family. We lift each other up. And that's what they did for me. I told them I have no clothes. They took me to a room where I could pick out what I want. Brand new underwear, brand new clothes, the tags still on them. I still have those clothes. A real coat. Jeans. They gave me toiletries. They gave me a bunk in the room. I said, this is my new beginning. I was secure. All I could do was go forward.

They gave me an opportunity to turn my life around. I got a physical. They fixed my teeth. Me and dentists don't get along, but they did my teeth. They greeted me with open arms, man! They welcomed me in. They set up a program where you can work and make some money while you're in this program. So, that's how I started working for the veterans' cemetery on Long Island. I would come home from working there, do pushups and lift weights. That was my recreation. We went to meetings. We laughed. I met a lot of great veterans. And staff. To this day, I still go to Northport, VA, even though I live in Pennsylvania to handle my physicals because they're family. They helped me get my life together. They pushed me, they believed in me when I was having some problems believing in myself.

Every time I go to the VA, I look for people to say hi. To see what happened to people who came in. Sometimes they want to go back to the old neighborhood to show them how they looked cleaned up. But they told us to stay away from people, places, and things of your old life, and that's real. That's not just a slogan. Because some people don't want you to succeed. Hey, buddy, hold something. They'll drink in front of you because they want you to come back to that side with them. To avoid that, just don't go on that side.

When I was there, I went to art class. I used to like drawing and sketching and doing things with a pencil. I did that there. This program was 35 – 40 days. Then they set up another program for me to go to. 64B—the guy that was in charge. He would come at you in a wrong way sometime. He kicked you in the butt, tough love, he didn't want you to come back. You'd say, I'm going to walk around this guy, I don't want to see him again. Telling me what to do.

Now, when I go to the VA, we're like best friends. We speak. We embrace each other. We used to bump heads. That's growth when you change your life. He said, I knew you could do it.

They had a room at the VA with clothes, and I wanted a suit, because I wanted to go to church and thank the Lord for changing my life. And I'm old school: You go to church, you dress up. You put on your Sunday best, put on a necktie. I wanted one of these suits.

Every Sunday I would walk to the water after church with my CD player. Take myself out to the elements. With the water and the jazz and myself. When I was in the "the life" you never had time to yourself, to look at yourself, because you're always just trying to stay alive.

Once I was sober, one of my friends told me I should go to the VA with him for music therapy. It helped him. They had contests and the winner got to travel to go national contests. Which sounded great to me. My first shows were in Northport, Long Island with the VA.

The VA is music therapy. We sing and compete.

By this time, I was sober and when they asked me to dance, I said, I don't know if I could. I need a taste to chase the butterflies.

Tracey Enright was my musical therapist at the Salvation Army, which had a program for veterans. In 2009, a brother told me to come and I did. This friend said he was going to California, all expenses paid, to compete there. I wasn't and still am not, a big singer. I dance, but they persuaded me to do a Louis Armstrong imitation doing "Hello Dolly." I won silver but wasn't invited to go to California. I said, "next year, I'm going to dance." So, in 2010, I competed. I did "Smooth Criminal." I went to LaCrosse, Wisconsin. That was my first big show. I got a standing ovation and I got hooked. Got the bug back. I went to Maryland and performed. I was hooked.

Then I was off to the races. I went to Wisconsin, Arkansas, Iowa, Reno. Drill team.

In New York once, I was dancing with a pole instead of a show rifle. A guy who did beautiful carving saw me and said, I have something for you. He carved me a wooden weapon. Then he carved me another.

The VA got me back on stage. For that I am eternally grateful, and for that reason I try to play it forward by helping my fellow veterans whenever I can.

This is what happened: I never danced without a "taste" to shoo the butterflies. But now, I was sober and determined to be so. I don't know what inspired me, but I went to a Party Supply Store and bought some white paint and smeared it all over my face. When I dance, I start kneeling with my head down. And this time, in white face, I had a funny feeling. I raised my head and shook it and I felt my body leave me and I jumped into the song "There Goes My Baby." This was at the National Veterans Creative Arts. It aired on PBS. Veterans from all over the US participated. They had more than 1,700 entries and only 100 were invited. That was the beginning.

Brad Howe, my veteran brother from another mother

Last year I celebrated 10 years being invited to the National Veteran's Creative Arts Festival. If anyone tells you that they can't change, tell them my story.

All gold at the National Veteran's Creative Arts Festival in Northport, LI

# CHAPTER 6

## You Never Know What You Can Do If You Don't Try

Ebn Ebn, owner of
Exquisite by Nature. I
perform at her lingerie
fashion show every year.

In 2011, doors opened up for me as a mime. Everyone asking me, "Can you do this or that song." I participated in "Stop the Violence." This lady used to work with me, we became friends. I performed at "National Night Against Crime" in Harlem. "Stop the Violence" in Harlem. One gig always leads to another. I started doing fashion shows in New York City with CMG. I open the show.

I did CMG fashion week last year. I've been performing for a decade. Doing mime since 2011.

Every year it gets bigger and bigger.

That doesn't mean that every door opened automatically. Like the day I went for *America Got Talent*. I couldn't believe I was going to audition for it. It was a 90 second audition, so you had to bring it

So that day, I drove to Philadelphia. I had butterflies the whole way. You get nervous when you know this might be something that will change your life for-ev-er. How would I feel if I made it past that first round. So, I'm thinking about the right song, how I'm going to play it.

My daughter dances as well, and she wanted to give it a shot as well. Both of us riding to Philadelphia on the edge of our seats. Both of us pumped, but not pumped nervous. We go in. Long line. It makes a wall. You want to get in, pump it out and get out, cause you're looking at that long long line.  All this talent. Everyone coming for the same thing. Hoping to get on TV. Hoping for the shot that will change your life forever. Never give up!

We run in, get out badges, sign in, get our wrist bands and now we're sitting in another big room.  They had different big rooms that were names. My daughter's nervous. I'm nervous. We're meeting people, networking. If we don't make it, at least we're networking, collaborating, whatever the case may be. Somebody might know somebody who knows somebody who likes what you do. Taking pictures. Getting yourself prepared.

Finally, your name is called. You go into a different room. You're in front of a desk with four guys. They're looking at you, expecting something. Butterflies. They're flying out of your ears. Different colors. And once the music starts, you switch gears. No more butterflies. You step into what you got to do. And I did it, man. I didn't get picked to go upstairs, where those that made it through that round went. But just giving it a shot, I won. To even be in the door, take pictures, to say I gave it shot, I won. I didn't go upstairs, but just auditioning, I won. *America Got Talent.* The guy who didn't know where his life was going to end up was auditioning for *America Got Talent.*

So, give it a shot man.

And if you don't get picked, you still won. You just got to go for it.

The Apollo. Early in the morning. First thing I got to find parking. Long line. They come down the line, giving out number. Early bird gets the worms. I parked my car and walked back with all my props. What I didn't know is that you only get 90 seconds. And it's hard to do mime, to show the story in 90 seconds. I picked a certain song, because I thought it would resonate with people in Harlem, "Dream" by Black.

But I got a number. Later on, I played the number. I said, if I don't get the job, I'll play the number. 197. It's still on my wall. Remember, the Apollo is where I used to ask for spare change, stinky, looking dirty. I used to look at it, and dream....*one day I want to dance in there.* I just want to walk in those doors one day. And what's crazy, now I'm auditioning, in the same place where I just dreamed of walking in the doors. I'm dancing!

You sit in a big auditorium; they call your name and you go into another auditorium in front of 4 judges. I did my thing. I didn't get picked. But I won. I got to dance in the Apollo.

One day, I might go back again. But for that one moment, I got the Grammy, the Oscar, the Academy Award, all rolled in one! I danced in the same place as the greats. James Brown. So, win or lose, if you give anything a shot, you WON, because it took initiative to do it.

I looked back at the door and a tear came to my eye, and I said, "I just danced in there." I might go back again, because you know my motto. "Never Give Up."

*America Got Talent*. Go for it! You want to go to the Olympics? Go for it! You want to be the best jumper? Go for it. You want to be the best runner? Go for it. Anything you want, go for it. Anything you go for, you win. There's a certain feeling when you go for something and dreaming. When they gave me that number 197. I took pictures like a won a Grammy.

I was with the *Dragon Squad* yesterday. A movie that I'm honored to be a part of and someone said, "Why don't you go for *America Got Talent?*" I said, "You know what? I did it before, but I'm thinking of doing it again." "Yeah, go for it!" I'm going to go for it again. You can't lose if you go for it.

You're never too old to do whatever it is you want to do. I always tell people, that you have to show up ready to perform, whatever your job is. Whether it's selling photo packages or airtime on the radio or putting on white face and dancing. Show up with your head in the game and looking good. Practice your moves.

CMG Helicopter photo shoot

# CHAPTER 7

Teaching Youth

Children are our future and our present.

One of the great joys of my life as a mime has been the opportunity to work with youth. I teach them through dance. The truth is that it doesn't matter what skill or art you teach kids, if you are teaching them a skill they respect and more importantly, if you respect them, they will listen and absorb all the lessons you have to teach them.

The thing I tell kids is that you'll run into walls. In fact, by the time I get them in a class, they have already hit a lot of walls. But don't let it take a toll on you. Take it as a lesson. When you hit a wall, lean on your higher power. Your passion! Your *juice*, like we talked about. It will take your mind off the wall and enable you to figure a way over that wall. Or you'll be able to see your way around it. Sometimes when you are able to take the emotion out of a situation—like confronting a big ole wall in your path—you can more calmly figure out what to do.

Listen, what I want to tell kids is, "You're not going to BELIEVE the stuff you'll have to go through!" Because all of us have been through some stuff. What I want to teach kids is how to focus, how to find a way to jump back on the path. And if you do let someone stop you, you'll feel the pain because you're not yourself.

Being yourself is the most important thing. You can't lose sight of that.

People will often disappoint you, because a lot of times what you want doesn't line up with what the other person wants. That's life, and it's actually normal. In fact, some of the people you say, "I love you" and they will flip real quick and say, "I dislike you." Sorry to say, that's pretty normal, too. When you reach someone at that point of intense emotion, it's easy to flip.

Even when someone flips like that, though, don't lose respect for people. Don't take it out on other people. When you do, it affects everyone around you, especially the people who love you.

Besides dancing, I work hard. I work 24/7. Sometimes, kids think that if they can't make enough money on their "juice" that it's not worth doing. No. it's what makes the other hard work make sense. I learned that when I was homeless. You still have all this energy, so you might as well put it to good use. You got to keep going. I have put a lot of work into negative stuff, I might as well put it into something positive. Every day when you're homeless you have to go to "work", the work being just staying alive on the streets.

I was working at the Sands Casino at that time and I had to work the night before so I get off of work at 10 o'clock in the morning and drive 8 hours to North Carolina in time for the show. When I finally get there, I took off my sunglasses and the host said, "wow, you look exhausted!" I was! But I performed, went to a friend's house to crash and got up and drove back to Pennsylvania for my next shift at Sands Casino. I wasn't paid for this event, but it was a good cause and I couldn't say no.

I always have this vision of my own funeral and what the people who are there are going to say. I don't want anyone to say, "that joker owes me $20!" I want to leave a legacy of inspiration. I want people to say, "he inspired me to be better, to do better." I want people to say "he always made me smile." Kids should always be thinking, "What am I leaving here? What am I creating?"

There are several organizations that I support. One is the Rilyc Community of the Arts Project. It was through Rilyc that I met Linda Vega. She was doing a gala for Rilyc. I danced to "Black." Linda and I got close and we did more events together, like at Touchstones.

Linda, who also works through Casa Guadeloupe, asked me if I wanted to do a mime and step routine project with her at Harrison Morton Middle School. We created dream books, other little projects with the kids before I taught them dance. My ex-manager didn't want me to work with the school district. He always wanted me to get paid, but as I said, if I believe in a cause I will do it for free. But the funny thing is, that now this program is getting funded.

The thing about working with kids is that you have to give 120%. All the time, all day. You got to show up when you say you're going to show up. If you say you're going to be there at 12 o'clock to teach them something, you'd better be there, because they'll be there waiting for you at the door. Maybe an hour before! The big reward is when the kids say, "You got some good moves for an old timer!"

I also support a program called "Cops and kids." One of the cops read "Three Little Pigs" and I mimed it. Huff and puff and blow your house down! One year a female military officer read a book that she wrote, and I mimed that too.

I love the kids. One kid liked to draw. She drew two pictures for me and autographed them then gave them to me. Another kid said, "I wish you were my big brother. I could travel with you and do shows." You don't know the impact you have.

That's why these two programs—Rilyc and Casa Guadaloupe—mean so much to me. They both let kids express themselves through art, because sometimes you don't have the words to tell people who you are. You need art, you need music, you need dance. You get confidence from performing or practicing your art. Even if you don't have the words, you always have your art.

Just ask me, I'm a mime!

# CHAPTER 8
COVID

In 2020 a virus from halfway around the world came and smacked us from behind and overtook us. We didn't know what hit us. One day I'm performing to crowds of people, the next day my daughter is home from school for the rest of the semester, I'm getting fitted for a face mask and wondering if I'll ever be able to put on mime makeup again.

Wow.

This is the time for thinking about my motto: Never give up!

I met a woman who flew into Pennsylvania from Arizona to see her father. Everyone told her she shouldn't. She was taking a big risk because of the virus. But she was determined. She said, "If I'm going to go down, I'm telling my mom, I saw my father first." I loved her determination. She wasn't giving up!

Sometimes you have to play through the pain. I think this Covid virus is one of those times. I was in a USAREUR competition in

Worms, Germany. I was enormously lucky to get a shot at it. The competition was like this: the first day was a show, the second day was competition, and the third day was another show. The first day, during the show, I twisted my ankle. It swelled up and I could hardly put my shoe on the next day. But this was the day of the competition! I had come too far to give up. In my act, smoke came up and I rise out of the smoke. I had a drink of wine, limped to the stage, got in position and when the smoke came up, I rose up and forgot about the pain and danced. I'm here! I said to myself.

After the show, a reporter for Armed Forces Network (AFN) came up to me and asked if he could interview me and of course I said, "Certainly!"

He said, "I saw you limping up to the stage, but then you got on stage and danced as if you were okay."

I told him, "I came too far to give up. I have to keep focusing on what I want and what I got to do to get there."

I think it's the same thing with Covid. Yeah, it's a setback in a lot of ways, but the world hasn't stopped turning. You got to keep moving. Take your vitamins. Wear your masks. Social distance. Do whatever it is you got to do to keep healthy while you keep moving forward. That way, when the virus has burned itself out, you're going to be ahead of where you would be if you just sat on the couch. It's going to work out.

I met a woman the other day. She was down. I tried to get her talking, to get her positive. She told me she was in a bad way.

"Ha!" I said. "Let me tell you a bit of my story!" Which I did.

She said, "Let me tell you something, mister. I'm going down. I'm out of money and I'm going to be homeless."

I told her, like I tell everyone, don't give up. You're a trooper. It's going to work out.

She was still sad when I left her. But I saw her again this morning. She was happy. She had gotten some funds. Now all she had to do was find a place to live.

"It's going to work out," I told her. "Sometimes you don't know how, and sometimes the how will surprise you, but you can never give up."

# CHAPTER 9
People Who Inspire Me!

Every show, every performance I've ever done is a blessing, and I've been dancing since I was a baby! I don't care if there's only one person in the audience.

At first, I would dance for my mom and her friends. They offered me fifty cents. Man, for fifty cents, I'd get myself together and dance. Then I would go to Mr. Boylan's store and get myself some penny candy. Ginger snaps. Mary Janes. Twizzlers. Taffy. Sugar Daddys and Sugar Babys. She would say, "Don't spend it all at the same time!" So she only gave me half at a time, but after I spend the first half, I'd run down and spend the second half.

I grew up watching Gene Kelley, Ginger Rogers, the Nicholas Brothers, Fred Astaire, Bill Robinson, Shirley Temple, Marcel Marceau, and Charlie Chaplin. I especially liked Charlie Chaplin, working with that cane. I was always grabbing his dance moves. I used to watch Soul Train to copy dance  moves too. Growing up in Virginia, we had battles in the playground. They called me "Robot." We'd be in a circle with a big old boombox on our shoulders. The best dancers would be out there. And we would dance and see who could out-dance everybody else. There was this one guy, who beat me every time. I wanted to beat him so bad. I thought I needed a gimmick. So, I walked home, cut all my hair off, came back with a hat on. They weren't ready for it. I started doing my robot moves and took off my hat. When they saw my bald head, everybody freaked out. It was intimidating! But it was fun. I got to be creative. I tried different things. Some things worked. Some things didn't. I got to hone my skills and my act.

I connected with a DJ and he would take me to Charleston to party. I would wear crutches into the club. I'd walk in like I was in pain, find myself a table and I'd sit there all night. Then the DJ would say, "I got a brother who can bring that song to life." And people would say, "He can't dance! He can't even walk!"

The DJ would pay me $50 to dance and if people liked what they saw, he gave me another $50. In the 1970s, this was a lot of money. I would sneak a couple sips of wine and go home and give my mama some money.

There was a Dance Club going on in downtown Richmond. $50 goes to the winner. Even though I was underage, I thought, "I got to get there!" So, at night, I snuck out the back door, figuring I could sneak back in. I met my friends and we went downtown to the contest. I danced. I had a ball! I came back home and snuck around the back, going slow so the dogs next door wouldn't bark when they heard me coming in, and…the back door is locked! I had to walk around the front. One of my uncles was waiting for me. He snatched me in. I never flew through the door that fast. I said, "I won $50!" He snatched the $50 from my hand and that was that.

I've had lots of good days dancing and they started getting really good when I met Tracey Enright. She worked at the Salvation Army in Northport, New York. Tracey is cool people. She had everyone singing and in drum circles. The buses don't run on Sunday in Sussex County, so I had a nice little walk to the water. I had my CD player with me, listening to jazz, sitting on the dock, watching the boats come in. That was my Sunday. I was trying to get my life back together.

Then I'd go to the Salvation Army in the VA . I was a dancer, but Tracey wanted me to sing. I could do a Louis Armstrong, "Hello Dolly!" and she said, "Great! Now we have something to work with." I said, why not? I'll do it for the veterans.

Then I entered the competition for the National Veterans Creative Arts Festival to be held in LaCrosse, Wisconsin that particular year. There were 7,000 entries for the 125 spots. Gold Medal Winners. And I was one! I just won a Gold Medal for doing something I loved.

I loved that scene in LaCrosse, Wisonsin. I saw the love the veterans showed each other. And you don't feel like you're going to work! I got up, went to breakfast, had a meeting, then rehearsal. Go to lunch, then rehearse. Go to dinner, then work on our vocals.

They definitely ran a tight ship. And I was hooked. The first time you get a standing ovation, you're hooked. You'll do anything for another one.

I went to La Crosse, Wisconsin to perform. Veterans from all over and every branch of service, every race and nationality. I think everyone should have to go in the military to experience that love.

The song I was dancing to was "My Baby." I was thinking, how can I interpret this, and I decided then, I'm going to do this as a mime. I went to Party Rental store and bought white paint—I didn't know what I was doing yet and just kind of smeared it on, no eyebrows or anything. But, when I came down the stairs, the crowd freaked out! It was a whole different look. I still wasn't sure until I saw the video, and that was it.

They asked me to come to Maryland and perform there. It was so dark in the theatre, I couldn't see the audience, so after I performed, I just went to the bathroom. My cousin, who was there to see me perform, came up to me and said, "Yo, man, you get a standing O!" I said, "Whaaaaat?????" It was a great feeling.

I started performing outside of the VA. I wanted to step out. But I had no email, no Facebook. I had a flip phone and a DVD player!

Finally, someone helped me set up and now I have 5,000 friends! I'm thankful for everyone who helped me get there and for helping me learn how to do it.

I got so much love and so many blessings from God, for which I will always be grateful. But still, I wouldn't change anything I had gone through, because then I wouldn't be the person I am today.

People ask me: You got a manager, you got an agent? I tell people now that God is my manager and my agent. I want a team that we just knock the roof off. But I just let God do it. I would do an event, seems like someone always says, give me a card, I think I have something for you, I think you would fit. And that's how I'd been going. I've been blessed to get these events. God is my manager. My life keeps on going forward. He got Bathsheba Monk in my life. She's helping me with my book. When I heard she's a veteran, it was like she's family. We knew each other for a thousand years.

I want to give a shout out to the many people who have helped me on my journey, who inspire me with love and talent and never give up!

- *URock Production*, an organization that does inspirational shows, gospel. Great group of people.
- Linda Vega, first time I did a show with her, we had talked on the phone several times. Her cousin Terry introduced me. I was working with Terry at Sands Casino. I was grinding. Some people talk, I was grinding. She finally said, I got someone I want you to meet. My cousin, Linda Vega. She's doing an

event and I'll tell her about you. Linda and I hit it off right away. I performed *Black* at the event.. I performed it for the kids at Black History Month. When I heard that song, I thought, I got to tell that story. That's what I did.

- Tuwanna Calpurnia, we did countless events. She does house gospel. She took me everywhere. I'm still working with her.

- I remember when I met my brother Stafford, at a fashion show in Manhattan. We connected. When I finished performing, he said, people are asking about you. He said, I have an event that I think you would fit right in. I want to stay in contact with you. We did selfies. He and his wife, Leah. Beautiful people. Real recognizes real. The event was about him proposing to Leah. We just sat back and cracked jokes. His whole family embraced me like they knew me a thousand years. And I'm there, just this mime dude, with white face. That's the kind of love the world needs to get hold of. I sat down and I was comfortable to a point where I told them I wore my shoes so much I had to put cardboard in the bottom to cover the holes and hope it don't rain that day. We cracked jokes about it, but it was real. That kind of stuff is when it happens, the after-party. The after-party is when you sit back and just kick it. I was honored to be part of that, honored to perform. His friends and family. Everybody. I'm not even talking about how much food we had! He's my brother. His wife, Leah, is my sister. Money can't buy that. He laughed at the holes in the shoes, because both of us could relate. The love I saw at that event, it went from a fashion show to seeing my brother get down on his knee and propose to his Leah. That's old school. Seeing two beautiful people get married. They're a powerful team. To witness it and be around it and feel it, is another blessing that money can't buy. Bob Marley says, it's a poor man who only has money. The Lord blesses me to be a millionaire, the Lord blesses me to have a penny, the Lord blesses me to have a brother like Stafford.

- TJ got a voice that will make you cry. I met her 2010. My first national, I was doing Michael Jackson "Smooth Criminal" in Lacrosse, Wisconsin. Veterans from all over the United States, Guam. All over. Alaska. Now I got friends in Alaska. Not going when it's cold though. TJ come out and say, "You got a light?" I said, "No, but come on, I'll walk with you." And we walked and talked. She's NY. I'm NY. We're kidding, laughing. We kicked it to the point where we became closer than close. She sings, she acts, she does it all. TJ would give you the shirt off her back. She's real. We're friends to this day. She's my sister from another mother. Family. Boy can she sing. Make you cry.

- Barry "Bee" played horn with Prince's band. How I met Barry: Driving an Uber. First time I picked him up it was pouring rain and I said "Yo bro, I'm going to tell you something, I don't drive fast in the rain, so I hope you're not in a rush to get somewhere." He said "No, I'd rather be safe than sorry." We kicked it and joked. I didn't know he was a performer. He didn't know I was a performer. We were just two guys kickin it in an Uber. I'm watching the road. Then I had to pick him up again. Some routine. Then it happened again and again. It was like I was his car! Then I said, "Yo, my man, let me tell you what I do. I perform. I dance and act. I try to take my art and inspire people." And then he told me who he was. "I played horn with Prince." And I said, "*Prince*, Prince?" and he said, "Yeah." "Wow. Respect." I asked him, how was it to perform for thousands of people? And he was the same dude I met the first time. I respected his art, but he was still that same dude. Barry "Bee" and I performed together at the SteelStacks at the Steampunk festival. They gave me 45 minutes, but that's long for a mime. As an example, once I was performing a Justin Timberlake song with Towanna that was 7 minutes. And I heard people saying, that's a long song, but he's keeping it going. So, I asked the SteelStacks people if I could bring some people with me, to showcase them, and they said yes, so I asked Barry "Bee." He said, "No problem. No problem." This guy who tours Europe, performs with George Benson, all the heavyweights. So, I got Barry "Bee," Linda Vega (spoken word) and Cindy Greatsinger. We did "Fever" and I mimed it. I performed 2 songs. "This is Me." This is a twist. Barry B and me did "Talk" we also performed Janet Jackson, "Sometime I Get Lonely." Linda Vega. Then me. "Ain't No Stopping Us

Now." We all got on stage together. I started dancing into the crowd and got people to dance, on the electric slide. The thing was, there was all walks of life there. That's what the world needs more of. We had EVERY nationality, all dancing together. That's how we closed the show out. That was a cool day, I'd do it again. That's what art is about.

When a person takes art and thinks money period, they throw the art away a little. Even though the Lord blessed me financially, I still want to do my free shows, hang with the youth, mingle with the crowd.

You hear about a lot of bad stuff going on, but when you hear about the good stuff, you got to hold it, you got to squeeze it. Keep it in your mind for when you need it. When I hear that crowd singing and dancing, "*there ain't no stopping us now.*" When I see my brother Stafford getting down on his knee proposing to his wife, Leah. When I hear TJ singing her song that made people cry in Lacrosse, Wisconsin, I see the love when all the veterans get together putting on a show and everyone's getting your bags and putting them on the truck, everyone's showing love from day one. All you're getting is love the whole time. Every year at a different location. That's the kind of love the world got to get.

I never dreamed I would be doing the things I'm doing, It's going to be alright. Remember that. The first day of school. You know who you were going to meet. Bullies. You know how school is. You're going to get an education. It's going to be alright. The first day on a job. You don't know what kind of people you're going to e working with. I signed this paper, I'm going to do this work and you're going to pay me this money. It's going to be alright.

When I worked at Sands, this guy says, Nate, you're always laughing and smiling.

I said, if you knew my story and I'm standing here talking to you, you'd be smiling too.

It's going to be alright.

# CHAPTER 10

## LEGENDS

I have been blessed to work with many talented and good people.

Daryl Dunkins, aka,
Chocolate Thumder

Big Red from the movie, *Five Heart Beats*

Wonder Mike, my Veteran brother, from the *Sugar Hill Gang*

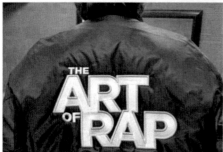

Michael McCue (DJ Solid Gold) and his wife, Millie Rivera

Jay R. Gomez (Magicus), third from left, and me opening for the legendary *Blue Magic* on Long Island.

Eleanore Mills

The legendary vocalist, Caleb T Johnson

Great vocalist Alicia Patterson

Me and the legendary Barry "Bee" performing at Steel Stacks

Performing for
Denise Boland's
television show,
*Remember This?*
Community
Television CTV,
Staten Island

Chrissy King
Bryant, Brooklyn
Mobile Tour,
giving me an
award

Randy Jones, the
original cowboy
from the *Village
People*

Uncle Ralph McDaniels, the man behind *Video Music Box*

Legendary vocalist, Carol Davis

Legendary Eban Brown

Khalilah Camacho Ali, Mohammed Ali's former wife

Linda Vega's All White Affair in Allentown, Pennsylvania

I perform at Lisa
Larkins (Lavish)
yacht parties.

TJ, my sister from another mother

Khalid Abdul Haqq Muhammad, son of one of the legendary *Ink Spots*. We were shooting a video that day.

Vida Isblessedallday Thomas and Queennasira Asantewaa Sekou, two sisters from another mother.

Anngeannette Pinkston, producer/director/wri ter of the movie, *Keys*, that I appeared in.

Video shoot with Monique Brown, singer/producer, second from left

Brother from another mother, Ronald Corbett Jr.

Legendary Stafford Chavis and his wife, Leah Chavis, my family forever

Legendary Jeff Redd

Marianne Ware from the legendary *Sweet Sensation*

Rhonda
Rock from
*URock
Productions*

The legendary Bill Godwin Ink Spots

Dr. Kitra Williams. In the famous Tyler Perry, "Diary of a Black Woman." Also, the legendary Ophra Winfrey play, "The Color Purple." I've been working with Dr. Williams from her AGAPE Awards and Million Youth March. I also performed with her and for her birthday on a cruise ship in the Bahamas.

Million Youth Peace March international, and "The Color Purple." We opened for the well-known Marvin Sapp.

Nate the Mime is honored to be featured in Grand Master
Tyrone Bullock's *Dragon Squad* film series with all the
amazing cast!

# CHAPTER 11
## The Best is Yet to Come

I sit back in the day, in the grocery store, thinking of what has been happening to me. I'm so thankful. I have two cars paid for—paid for! —in my driveway. I was homeless. I had nothing. Holey shoes. I was dirty, stinking. I'm so thankful to be able to be even able to perform and meet so many blessed people. It's not about the money, yes of course I am thankful for the financial blessings that have been coming in, I'm thankful just to be able to walk the streets like a normal citizen of the United States and the world! But I'm thankful more for just having this feeling. I'm not where I want to be yet, but I'm way better than I was before. And I'm so thankful. I would love to be in the position to bless other people financially, put some homeless houses up, put an art building for artists to do their art, I want to be televised so I can tell people, "Dreams still come true." I wanted to be a known dancer like I used to watch when I was a kid. I always wanted that. But my journey took me around so I was military and homeless and now I want to use all this stuff to say, no matter how old you are, it can happen. Something good can happen. Forget the fame, if fame comes with it that's cool, but I want to be blessed. So, I can inspire someone to keep driving no matter how old, how young, or no matter what people might say. Or maybe they'll say, oh my God, I'm late to this, maybe I should just give up. No, you got to keep going. I just want you to keep going, man. That's what I'm doing. You never know what's behind a door. So, if a blessing come up, like sometimes I perform for money, sometimes I perform for free.

Cause you never know what's behind that door. You never know if it's for you. You can't say, oh, I want a thousand dollars. No, just go in the door. That could be the blessing that's waiting for you. So just go in. That's what I want the world to know.

You heart is what makes you. Yeah, you need money for cars and houses and paying bills, but it's your heart that makes you. Your spirit. Bob Marley said, "A poor man only has money."

Tyler Perry, Oprah Winfrey, I want to meet those people who are blessing other people. I want to meet them. I want to be around their energy, and I want to thank them. Anybody who's inspiring, they don't have to be famous. I enjoy meeting people who are doing great things for the world. Neighborhood, community. We need those things. So anytime anyone calls me, I don't hesitate. My schedule's clear, let's do it, let's go. Egypt? Let's do this. Because we got to give people platforms to do their thing. I want to always make the choice to do something, not to NOT do something. And I want to keep on doing these. Keep on being inspired. We all got to be hooked up. We're all going through situations where we think, I don't know if I'm going to make it, and we need someone to come up and say, "You got this, man, you're a trooper, you can do this."

That's one thing my grandmother always taught. You can always be kind, even if the other person isn't. One of the nicest things anyone ever said about wasn't about my dancing or my miming or anything like that. It was Chris Steinert, a man I sat next to on a job orientation.

> *"I worked with this man, Nate Moran, at my last job. He sat next to me in orientation. The man always had a smile on his face and stayed positive. This man is a performer and is destined for fame, but this image struck me because there is so much chaos going on in the world and yet Nate is positive. We come across amazing people in life and Nate is one of those people. He is someone I strive to be. Stay loving and positive."*

Every action has a reaction. The more you give, the more you get. If people aren't nice to you, still be kind.

And of course, Never Give Up.

# ABOUT THE AUTHOR

Nate Moran, aka Nate the Mime, performs his art all over the world. See more about him at www.natethemime.com

Made in the USA
Middletown, DE
08 January 2021

30774302R00058